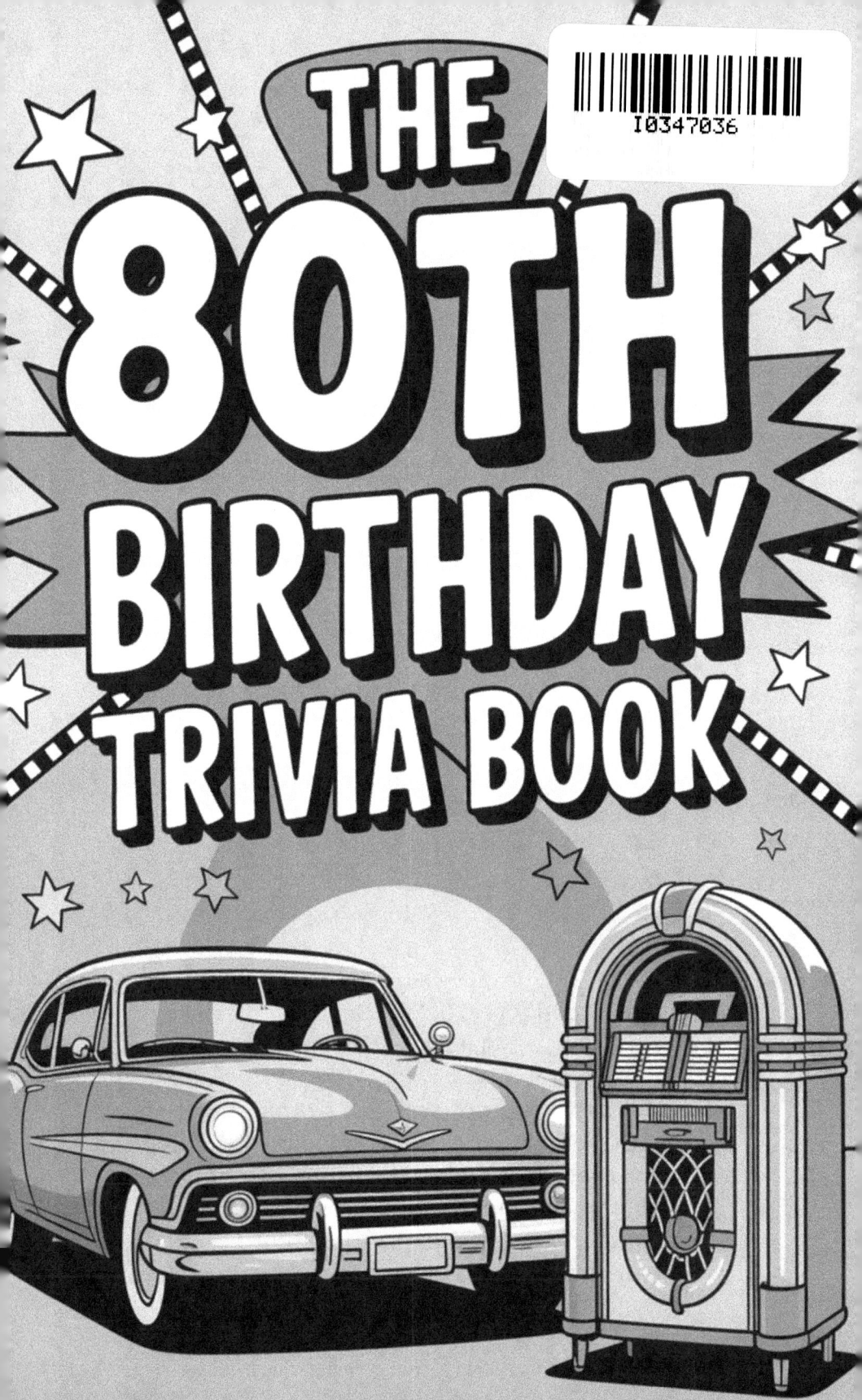

Copyright © 2025 by Scott Matthews
All rights reserved.

No part of this publication may be reproduced, stored in a retrieval system, or transmitted in any form or by any means, including electronic, mechanical, photocopying, recording, or otherwise, without the prior written permission of the publisher, except in the case of brief quotations used in reviews or scholarly works.

CONTENT

INTRODUCTION..1
CHAPTER 1...3
   Everyday Life in the '40s–'60s.................................4
   Answers...11
   Did You Know?..13

CHAPTER 2..14
   Classic TV Shows and Movies...................................15
   Answers..21
   Did You Know?...24

CHAPTER 3..25
   On the Radio: Vintage Music & Bands.....................26
   Answers..33
   Did You Know?...36

CHAPTER 4..37
   History Highlights..38
   Answers..44
   Did You Know?...47

CHAPTER 5..48
   Gadgets & Tech...49
   Answers..55
   Did You Know?...58

CHAPTER 6 59
   Sports Legends of the Past............................... 60
   Answers... 66
   Did You Know?... 69

CHAPTER 7.. 70
   Retro Toys and Games....................................... 71
   Answers... 77
   Did You Know?... 80

CHAPTER 8.. 81
   School Days.. 82
   Answers... 88
   Did You Know?... 91

CHAPTER 9.. 92
   Famous People... 93
   Answers... 99
   Did You Know?..102

CHAPTER 10..103
   Food and Drink..104
   Answers... 110
   Did You Know?... 113
CONCLUSION.. 114

INTRODUCTION

Can you believe it? You're turning eighty, or maybe you just did. That's eighty years of memories, milestones, and moments that have made life full and meaningful. From riding bikes and listening to the radio to raising a family and watching the world change, you've seen and experienced so much. What a beautiful journey it's been.

You've lived through times of great change. You remember when phones had cords, milk was delivered to your doorstep, and kids played outside until the streetlights came on. You've seen the first steps on the moon, the rise of color TV, and the world go from handwritten letters to text messages. Through it all, you've kept learning, growing, and living with heart.

That's what this book is here to celebrate. This is your 80th Birthday Trivia Challenge, filled with fun and thoughtful questions to help you look back and smile. Inside, you'll find ten chapters with twenty questions each, covering everything from music and movies to history, inventions, and everyday life.

Each chapter also includes a "Did You Know?" section with surprising facts that might spark a memory or teach you something new.

You don't need to know all the answers. This book is for enjoying the ride. You can play along with family and friends or take your time on your own. Share stories, laugh at the memories, and enjoy thinking back on the moments that helped shape who you are.

So go ahead, grab a pen and get cozy. Let's celebrate eighty wonderful years with fun, laughter, and love. This is your time, and this is your story to remember and enjoy.

Happy Birthday!

Everyday Life in the '40s-'60s

Life in the 1940s, '50s, and early '60s was a mix of simplicity, tradition, and big changes. Families gathered around radios before TVs took center stage. Kids played outside until the streetlights came on. You got your milk from the milkman, your news from the newspaper, and your music from a jukebox or record player. People dressed up to go to the movies, and fast food was just starting to take off. It was a time of penny candy, rotary phones, and backyard barbecues.

How much do you remember, or how much do you think you know about everyday life back then? Let's find out with these fun, nostalgic multiple-choice trivia questions!

1. Back in the 1950s, the kitchen was the heart of the home, and new appliances were making life easier. Which one of these handy machines started becoming a staple in American kitchens during that time, revolutionizing food preparation and saving housewives time and effort?

a) Toaster oven
b) Dishwasher
c) Electric mixer
d) Garbage disposal

2. Women's hairstyles in the 1960s were as bold as the decade itself. Which iconic, towering hairdo was all the rage, often requiring hours of teasing and hairspray to achieve that unmistakable look?

a) Bob cut
b) Beehive
c) Pixie cut
d) French twist

3. Color television was a huge breakthrough in the 1950s, bringing living rooms to life with vibrant images. Which popular event was the first color broadcast in the U.S., dazzling viewers with its vivid spectacle?

a) *The Ed Sullivan Show*
b) *I Love Lucy*
c) *The Tournament of Roses Parade*
d) *The Andy Griffith Show*

4. Cars were symbols of freedom and prosperity in the early 1950s. What was the average price tag for a brand- new car back then — a price that many American families dreamed of saving up for?

a) $500
b) $1,500
c) $3,000
d) $5,000

5. Convenience foods were on the rise, changing the way families ate dinner. Which of these popular snack foods made its debut in 1953 and quickly became a household favorite?

a) Cheetos
b) Cheez Whiz
c) TV dinner
d) Doritos

6. Telephones in the 1940s looked very different from today's smartphones. Which type of phone was the most common in homes during that era, the one with a dial that you had to turn to call someone?

a) Touch-tone tabletop phone
b) Candlestick crank phone
c) Rotary dial telephone
d) Wall-mounted payphone

7. Before refrigeration became widespread in grocery stores and supermarkets, how did many families

receive their fresh dairy products like milk and cream on a regular basis?

a) Weekly pickup at a local dairy barn
b) Home delivery by a uniformed service worker
c) Through refrigerated compartments in grocery trucks
d) Subscription boxes from local general stores

8. Fashion in the '50s had its playful side. Which popular clothing item, named after a certain four-legged friend, twirled its way into teenage closets across the country?

a) Ponytail scarf
b) Poodle skirt
c) Cat-eye glasses
d) Leopard print top

9. In the early 1950s, a children's novelty item was released that encouraged imaginative expression by allowing youngsters to accessorize household produce with interchangeable plastic features. Originally sold without the "body" included, it required kids to supply their own vegetables. Which product fits this peculiar origin?

a) Hasbro's Spud Buddy Kit
b) VeggieMates Decoration Set
c) Mr. Potato Head Parts Pack
d) Tater Tot Play Bundle

10. Long before streaming or digital downloads, what type of music player was a common fixture in American homes during the 1960s?

a) Cassette player
b) 8-track
c) Record player
d) MP3

11. Lunchboxes from the 1950s often held simple but tasty meals. Which of these classic lunch items would you most likely find inside a child's lunchbox back then?

a) String cheese and a Capri Sun
b) Peanut butter and jelly sandwich
c) Sliced deli wrap with ranch dip
d) Pre-packaged fruit snacks

12. Kids in the 1940s and '50s helped out with simple chores around the house. Which task was commonly assigned to children to keep the household running smoothly?

a) Programming the electric thermostat
b) Scheduling calls on the rotary phone
c) Filling the metal ice cube tray in the freezer
d) Logging chores into the family calendar app

13. Car colors in the 1950s could be quite vivid. Which color was the most popular choice for new cars in that decade — a fun and fresh hue that stood out on

the road?

a) Red
b) Yellow
c) Aqua
d) Silver

14. Writing instruments evolved through the decades. What type of pen became widely used in the 1950s, replacing older styles and making everyday writing easier and cleaner?

a) Fountain pen
b) Quill pen
c) Ballpoint pen
d) Felt-tip pen

15. Saturday mornings were a sacred time for many kids in the 1960s. What activity was a beloved ritual that kids looked forward to all week?

a) Listening to radio soap operas
b) Watching black-and-white cartoons
c) Attending early piano lessons
d) Helping parents wash the car

16. Some candies hold a special place in history. Which chocolate treat, introduced in 1941, became a favorite among soldiers during World War II for its durability and taste?

a) M&M's

b) Skittles
c) Jolly Ranchers
d) Nerds

17. Teenage boys in the 1950s often showed their school spirit and style with a particular type of jacket. Which one was a staple for high school jocks and cool kids alike?

a) Varsity sweater
b) Bomber jacket
c) Letterman jacket
d) Denim trucker jacket

18. Home heating in the 1940s looked very different from today's systems. What was a common way households stayed warm during chilly months?

a) Electric baseboard heaters
b) Solar heating
c) Coal or wood-burning stove
d) Radiant floor heating

19. Dance crazes often defined the social scene. Which energetic and twisting dance became wildly popular in the late 1950s, inspiring countless parties and sock hops?

a) The Twist
b) Macarena
c) Electric Slide
d) The Hand Jive

20. Advertisements in the 1950s had catchy slogans that stuck with consumers. Which phrase became famous for a household cleaner, warning about stubborn laundry stains?

a) "Plink it clean!"
b) "Nothing cleans like bleach!"
c) "Look, Ma—no hands!"
d) "Ring Around the Collar"

CHAPTER 1 ANSWERS

1. <u>c) Electric mixer</u> – The electric mixer made baking and cooking faster and less tiring, becoming essential in many households.

2. <u>b) Beehive</u> – Its towering style defined 1960s fashion and required lots of hairspray.

3. <u>c) The Tournament of Roses Parade</u> – The parade's colorful floats were perfect for showcasing the new color TV technology.

4. <u>b) $1,500</u> – Around $1,500 was the typical cost, making cars a major but attainable investment.

5. <u>c) TV dinner</u> – The TV dinner introduced easy-to-prepare meals, perfect for the busy 1950s household.

6. <u>c) Rotary dial telephone</u> – The rotary dial phone required users to turn a numbered dial for each call.

7. <u>b) Home delivery by a uniformed service worker</u> – The milkman delivered fresh milk directly to doorsteps daily or weekly.

8. <u>b) Poodle skirt</u> – This skirt was a flared felt skirt decorated with a poodle applique — a teen favorite.

9. <u>c) Mr. Potato Head Parts Pack</u> – Mr. Potato Head was sold as parts only at first, requiring kids to use a real potato.

10. c) Record player - The main device for playing music on vinyl records.

11. c) Peanut butter and jelly sandwich - Simple, tasty, and easy to pack for school lunches.

12. c) Filling the metal ice cube tray in the freezer - Kids often helped by filling ice trays by hand to keep drinks cold.

13. c) Aqua - Aqua was a trendy and eye-catching color on many '50s cars.

14. c) Ballpoint pen - Ballpoint pens became affordable and convenient alternatives to fountain pens.

15. b) Watching black-and-white cartoons - Saturday morning cartoons were a special weekly treat for children.

16. a) M&M's - M&M's were included in soldiers' rations because they didn't melt easily.

17. c) Letterman jackets - They symbolized school pride and athletic achievement, making them a must-have for teen athletes in the 1950s.

18. c) Coal or wood-burning stove - Many homes relied on stoves burning coal or wood for heat.

19. a) The Twist - The Twist was a simple yet fun dance that swept the nation in the late '50s.

20. d) "Ring Around the Collar" - This slogan warned about tough shirt stains caused by sweat and dirt.

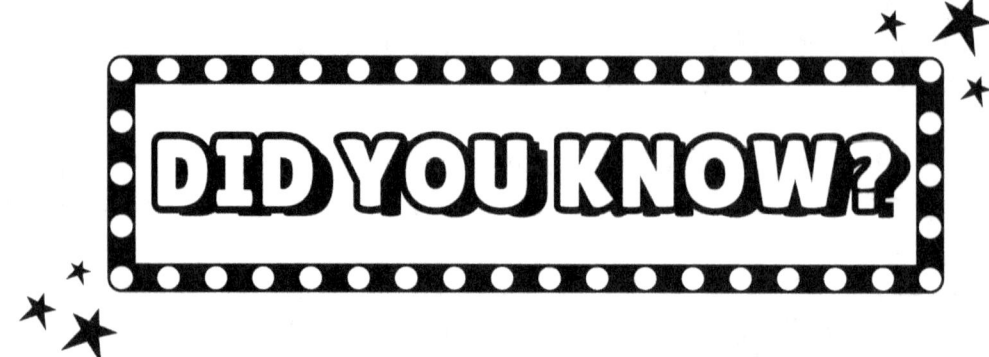

Did you know that before the invention of the modern credit card, many people in the 1950s used "charge plates," small metal cards with their names and account numbers embossed on them? These plates were swiped at stores to keep track of purchases before the magnetic stripe cards we know today even existed!

Did you know that soda fountains were a social hotspot in the 1940s and '50s, where teens would gather to sip on milkshakes, root beer floats, and sundaes? These colorful soda shops were often the place to see and be seen, kind of like today's coffee shops or food courts.

The "TV dinner" wasn't just about convenience but also about marketing a new lifestyle centered around television watching. The first TV dinners were sold in metal trays and featured classic American meals like turkey, mashed potatoes, and peas, all designed for easy reheating and eating while enjoying your favorite shows.

Classic TV Shows and Movies

From the golden days of Hollywood to the heyday of black-and-white television, the screen has given us some of the most unforgettable moments in pop culture history. Whether it was a night at the movies or tuning in to your favorite weekly show, these stories became part of everyday life. So grab your popcorn and settle in, because this round is all about the classic shows and silver screen legends that defined generations.

1. That unforgettable line, "Here's looking at you, kid" has become one of cinema's most iconic quotes. But which classic 1942 film gave us this charming farewell?

a) *Casablanca*
b) *Citizen Kane*
c) *The Maltese Falcon*
d) *Gone with the Wind*

2. Imagine being the very first audience to watch a full-length animated fairy tale back in 1937. Which groundbreaking Walt Disney film introduced this magical milestone to movie lovers everywhere?

a) *Cinderella*
b) *Snow White and the Seven Dwarfs*
c) *Sleeping Beauty*
d) *Fantasia*

3. Which 1959 film, known for its breathtaking chariot races and epic storytelling, was directed by William Wyler and won a record-setting eleven Academy Awards?

a) *Lawrence of Arabia*
b) *Ben-Hur*
c) *The Ten Commandments*
d) *The Searchers*

4. In 1981, audiences were introduced to a daring archaeologist who'd steal hearts and artifacts alike.

Which adventurous film first brought Indiana Jones and his iconic fedora to the big screen?

a) *Raiders of the Lost Ark*
b) *Indiana Jones and the Temple of Doom*
c) *Indiana Jones and the Last Crusade*
d) *Indiana Jones and the Kingdom of the Crystal Skull*

5. "I'm gonna make him an offer he can't refuse" is a line that echoes through movie history. Which gripping 1972 crime drama featured this unforgettable threat?

a) *Goodfellas*
b) *The Godfather*
c) *Scarface*
d) *The Godfather Part II*

6. Picture the suspense of a small beach town suddenly terrorized by a massive, toothy predator in 1975. What blockbuster movie introduced audiences to the ultimate summer thriller about a killer shark?

a) *Deep Blue Sea*
b) *The Deep*
c) *Jaws*
d) *Shark Attack*

7. Who brought to life the gentle, slow-witted hero in the 1994 film that took us on a journey through decades of American history, love, and fate?

a) John Travolta
b) Robin Wright
c) Gary Sinise
d) Tom Hanks

8. The legendary phrase "May the Force be with you" first ignited the imaginations of sci-fi fans in which 1977 space adventure film?

a) *Star Wars: A New Hope*
b) *Star Wars: The Empire Strikes Back*
c) *Star Wars: Return of the Jedi*
d) *Star Trek*

9. In 1997, a sweeping romantic drama told the story of a doomed luxury liner's tragic maiden voyage, blending historical disaster with unforgettable love. Which film captured this epic tale on the big screen?

a) *Titanic*
b) *The Poseidon Adventure*
c) *A Night to Remember*
d) *Ghost Ship*

10. Which mythical sea creature plays a major role as a terrifying adversary in *Pirates of the Caribbean: Dead Man's Chest*?

a) Kraken
b) Leviathan
c) Sea Serpent
d) Charybdis

11. The very first James Bond film introduced audiences to the suave British spy in 1962. What was the title of this thrilling debut?

a) *Goldfinger*
b) *Dr. No*
c) *From Russia with Love*
d) *Casino Royale*

12. This 1939 epic drama swept the Oscars with its sweeping romance and stunning visuals. Which film became the first of that year to win Best Picture?

a) *The Grapes of Wrath*
b) *Rebecca*
c) *Gone with the Wind*
d) *How Green Was My Valley*

13. In Disney's 1994 animated classic, which wise and quirky meerkat serves as one of the loyal friends guiding the young lion prince on his journey?

a) Timon
b) Pumbaa
c) Zazu
d) Rafiki

14. Which visionary director stunned audiences with thrilling dinosaur adventures in the groundbreaking 1993 film *Jurassic Park*?

a) Steven Spielberg

b) James Cameron
c) George Lucas
d) Ridley Scott

15. Which hit song from the *Grease* soundtrack became an anthem for youthful rebellion and was famously performed by John Travolta and Olivia Newton-John?

a) "You're the One That I Want"
b) "Stayin' Alive"
c) "Footloose"
d) "Fame"

16. In the heartwarming 1982 film *E.T. the Extra-Terrestrial*, what candy does the lovable alien use to fuel his otherworldly friendship?

a) Reese's Pieces
b) M&M's
c) Skittles
d) Hershey's Kisses

17. Batman fans everywhere were thrilled when this 2008 film brought the Dark Knight to life in a gripping battle against the Joker. What was the film?

a) *Batman Begins*
b) *The Dark Knight*
c) *Batman Forever*
d) *Batman & Robin*

18. The chilling thriller *The Silence of the Lambs* earned which actress the Best Actress Oscar in 1991 for her portrayal of Clarice Starling?

a) Jodie Foster
b) Julianne Moore
c) Meryl Streep
d) Nicole Kidman

19. Which 1946 noir film stars Humphrey Bogart as private detective Philip Marlowe, navigating a web of mystery and danger?

a) *The Big Sleep*
b) *Double Indemnity*
c) *Chinatown*
d) *The Maltese Falcon*

20. Featuring timeless songs like "Do-Re-Mi" and "My Favorite Things," which 1965 musical captured the hearts of audiences around the world?

a) *The Sound of Music*
b) *West Side Story*
c) *Mary Poppins*
d) *Singin' in the Rain*

CHAPTER 2 ANSWERS

1. <u>a)</u> <u>*Casablanca*</u> - This 1942 classic made "Here's looking at you, kid" one of Hollywood's most quoted lines.

2. <u>b)</u> <u>*Snow White and the Seven Dwarfs*</u> - It was the first full-length animated feature film, released by Disney in 1937.

3. <u>b)</u> <u>*Ben-Hur*</u> - The epic film won eleven Oscars and is famous for its intense chariot race scene.

4. <u>a)</u> <u>*Raiders of the Lost Ark*</u> - This 1981 blockbuster introduced Indiana Jones and redefined the action-adventure genre.

5. <u>b)</u> <u>*The Godfather*</u> - This iconic 1972 crime film is known for its memorable quotes and mafia storyline.

6. <u>c)</u> <u>*Jaws*</u> - Steven Spielberg's 1975 thriller made people afraid to go back in the water.

7. <u>d)</u> <u>Tom Hanks</u> - He portrayed Forrest Gump, whose simple outlook offered deep lessons about life and history.

8. <u>a)</u> <u>*Star Wars: A New Hope*</u> - The phrase "May the Force be with you" originated in the 1977 sci-fi phenomenon.

9. a) *Titanic* - Released in 1997, *Titanic* blended real-life tragedy with fictional romance, becoming one of the highest-grossing and most beloved films of all time.

10. a) Kraken - This monstrous sea creature was Davy Jones' terrifying weapon in *Dead Man's Chest*.

11. b) *Dr. No* - The first James Bond film starred Sean Connery and kicked off a legendary franchise.

12. c) *Gone with the Wind* - This Civil War-era drama won Best Picture and became a cultural and box office milestone.

13. a) Timon - He's the wisecracking meerkat who helps Simba in *The Lion King*.

14. a) Steven Spielberg - He directed *Jurassic Park*, bringing dinosaurs to life through groundbreaking CGI (computer-generated imagery).

15. a) "You're the One That I Want" - This electrifying duet became one of the most iconic songs from *Grease*.

16. a) Reese's Pieces - E.T.'s love for this candy helped boost its popularity after the film's release.

17. b) *The Dark Knight* - Heath Ledger's Joker and Christian Bale's Batman made this 2008 film a modern classic.

18. a) Jodie Foster - Her portrayal of Clarice Starling in *The Silence of the Lambs* won her a Best Actress Oscar.

19. a) *The Big Sleep* - Humphrey Bogart played

detective Philip Marlowe in this twisty 1946 noir film.

20. a) *The Sound of Music* - This beloved musical told the story of the von Trapp family and featured iconic songs.

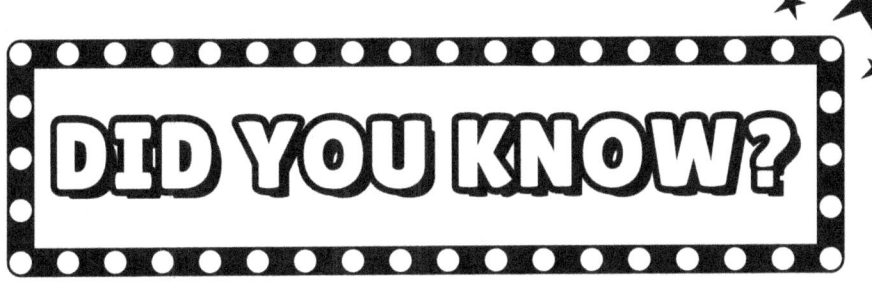

When Walt Disney released *Snow White and the Seven Dwarfs* in 1937, it was the very first full-length animated feature ever created. Many critics called it "Disney's folly," thinking audiences wouldn't sit through an hour and a half of cartoons. But the movie was a huge success and proved animation could be a serious art form, forever changing Hollywood.

Indiana Jones' fedora hat wasn't just a costume piece; it almost got destroyed several times during daring stunt scenes. The prop masters took special care to preserve it because it became a symbol of the adventurous archaeologist's identity. Harrison Ford's iconic look was partly defined by that signature hat.

During the filming of *Jaws*, the mechanical shark, nicknamed "Bruce," kept breaking down, forcing director Steven Spielberg to use the shark sparingly and rely more on suspense and the fear of the unknown. This unexpected challenge ended up making the film scarier, as audiences feared what they couldn't see.

On the Radio: Vintage Music & Bands

Long before streaming and playlists, the radio was king. From toe-tapping tunes of the '40s to the rock 'n' roll explosion of the '60s, music filled homes, jukeboxes, and dance halls with unforgettable sound.

Turn up the dial, this round takes you back to the golden age of music, where big bands, crooners, and chart-toppers ruled the airwaves.

1. Before playlists and podcasts, millions tuned into radio waves to hear smooth vocals and swoon-worthy melodies. Known for his velvet voice and charismatic charm, which iconic singer earned the nickname "The Chairman of the Board" during the height of the Big Band and swing era?

a) Nat King Cole
b) Bing Crosby
c) Dean Martin
d) Frank Sinatra

2. Which Beatles song is widely believed to have been inspired by a dream Paul McCartney had and originally carried the working title "Scrambled Eggs"?

a) Blackbird
b) Yesterday
c) I'm Only Sleeping
d) Golden Slumbers

3. This legendary guitarist, known for his fiery solos and wild stage presence, made an explosive impact on the late '60s rock scene despite a tragically short career. Who was he?

a) Eric Clapton
b) Jimmy Page
c) Jimi Hendrix
d) Jeff Beck

4. The Motown sound brought unforgettable artists to

the forefront of the American music scene. Which singer was famously crowned the "Queen of Motown"?

a) Diana Ross
b) Aretha Franklin
c) Martha Reeves
d) Gladys Knight

5. Before the Beatles dominated, this "King of Rock and Roll" shook the world with his hip-swinging moves and powerful voice. Who was he?

a) Jerry Lee Lewis
b) Elvis Presley
c) Carl Perkins
d) Roy Orbison

6. This theatrical anthem by Queen, known for its operatic structure, dramatic shifts in tempo, and cryptic lyrics, became one of the most iconic rock songs of all time. Which track are we talking about?

a) Somebody to Love
b) Bohemian Rhapsody
c) We Are the Champions
d) Radio Ga Ga

7. Known as the "King of Soul," this artist's emotional vocals helped change the sound of American R&B forever. Who was he?

a) Marvin Gaye

b) Curtis Mayfield
c) James Brown
d) Sam Cooke

8. This influential folk artist rose to prominence in the 1960s, captivating audiences with thought-provoking lyrics and a raw, unconventional vocal style. His early work, including a song that questioned war and freedom, became deeply associated with the civil rights movement. Who was he?

a) Bob Dylan
b) Joan Baez
c) Pete Seeger
d) Woody Guthrie

9. The Beach Boys shifted from surf tunes to more sophisticated sounds in the mid-1960s. Which 1966 album is widely praised for its innovation and is often ranked among the greatest albums of all time?

a) *Surfin' USA*
b) *Pet Sounds*
c) *Endless Summer*
d) *Smile*

10. She lit up the disco era with a powerhouse anthem of resilience and independence. Which artist's 1978 hit became a defining song of the genre and a lasting symbol of empowerment?

a) Donna Summer

b) Gloria Gaynor
c) Diana Ross
d) Evelyn "Champagne" King

11. Celebrated for his gravelly voice, innovative trumpet solos, and pioneering scat singing, this jazz icon helped bring the genre into the mainstream and became a global ambassador for American music. Who was he?

a) Miles Davis
b) Louis Armstrong
c) Duke Ellington
d) Charlie Parker

12. Known for her powerful voice and emotional ballads, which singer earned the nickname "Lady Soul"?

a) Aretha Franklin
b) Etta James
c) Tina Turner
d) Billie Holiday

13. Often credited with capturing the restless spirit of the 1960s, this 1965 Rolling Stones hit became an anthem of frustration and rebellion, opening with one of the most recognizable guitar riffs in rock history. Which song is it?

a) Paint It Black
b) (I Can't Get No) Satisfaction

c) Jumpin' Jack Flash
d) Time Is on My Side

14. Which legendary band's 1969 album *Abbey Road* featured the famous cover of the band walking across a zebra crossing in London?

a) The Beatles
b) The Rolling Stones
c) The Who
d) The Kinks

15. Known for his slicked-back hair and energetic dance moves, this 1950s star's hits include "Great Balls of Fire" and "Whole Lotta Shakin' Goin' On." Who was he?

a) Jerry Lee Lewis
b) Elvis Presley
c) Little Richard
d) Chuck Berry

16. The 1960s saw the rise of psychedelic rock. Which band is famous for the album *The Piper at the Gates of Dawn* and the song "See Emily Play"?

a) Pink Floyd
b) The Doors
c) Jefferson Airplane
d) The Byrds

17. Which female singer became the voice of the 1960s

civil rights movement with powerful songs like "Respect" and "Think"?

a) Aretha Franklin
b) Nina Simone
c) Mahalia Jackson
d) Billie Holiday

18. In the early '70s, this English rock band created a mythic fantasy world through their album *Thick as a Brick*, often considered a masterpiece of progressive rock. Who are they?

a) Genesis
b) Yes
c) Jethro Tull
d) King Crimson

19. Before becoming a solo superstar, this legendary singer was the lead vocalist for the band The Temptations. Who was he?

a) Stevie Wonder
b) Marvin Gaye
c) David Ruffin
d) Smokey Robinson

20. Which American folk rock band, famous for hits like "Mr. Tambourine Man" and "Turn! Turn! Turn!," helped popularize folk music with electric instruments in the mid-1960s?

a) The Byrds
b) Simon & Garfunkel
c) The Mamas & the Papas
d) Crosby, Stills, Nash & Young

CHAPTER 3 ANSWERS

1. <u>d) Frank Sinatra</u> - Sinatra was famously dubbed "The Chairman of the Board" as a nod to both his leadership in the music world and his founding role in Reprise Records.

2. <u>b) Yesterday</u> - Paul McCartney composed "Yesterday" from a melody he dreamed, originally calling it "Scrambled Eggs."

3. <u>c) Jimi Hendrix</u> - Jimi Hendrix electrified the rock world with his innovation and raw energy, cementing his legacy in just a few short years.

4. <u>a) Diana Ross</u> - Diana Ross rose to fame as the lead singer of The Supremes and became Motown's biggest female star, earning the title "Queen of Motown."

5. <u>b) Elvis Presley</u> - Elvis Presley's explosive rise in the mid-1950s reshaped music and pop culture, making him an enduring icon of early rock and roll.

6. b<u>) Bohemian Rhapsody</u> - This Queen hit is known for its operatic shifts, theatrical structure, and enduring popularity.

7. <u>c) James Brown</u> - Though often called the "Godfather of Soul," Brown's influence and style also earned him the title "King of Soul."

8. <u>a) Bob Dylan</u> - Dylan's poetic lyrics and protest

song became anthems of the civil rights and antiwar movements.

9. a) *Pet Sounds* - The Beach Boys' *Pet Sounds* revolutionized pop production and inspired artists worldwide with its layered sound.

10. b) Gloria Gaynor - Her 1978 hit "I Will Survive" became an enduring anthem of strength, especially during the disco era.

11. b) Louis Armstrong - Armstrong's iconic gravelly voice and trumpet helped bring jazz to mainstream America.

12. a) Aretha Franklin - Her unmatched vocals and soulful anthems earned her the nickname "Lady Soul."

13. b) (I Can't Get No) Satisfaction - The Stones' gritty anthem voiced '60s frustration, anchored by one of rock's most famous riffs.

14. a) The Beatles - The *Abbey Road* album cover became one of the most iconic images in music history.

15. a) Jerry Lee Lewis - His wild piano playing and hits like "Great Balls of Fire" made him a rock 'n' roll pioneer.

16. a) Pink Floyd - Their debut album and songs like "See Emily Play" helped shape the psychedelic rock genre.

17. a) Aretha Franklin - Songs like "Respect" became soundtracks for empowerment and civil rights activism.

18. c) Jethro Tull - Their concept album *Thick as a Brick* showcased storytelling and complexity in progressive rock.

19. c) David Ruffin - Known for his lead on "My Girl," Ruffin's powerful vocals defined The Temptations' biggest hits.

20. a) The Byrds - Their fusion of folk and rock gave birth to a new sound and redefined the genre in the mid-1960s.

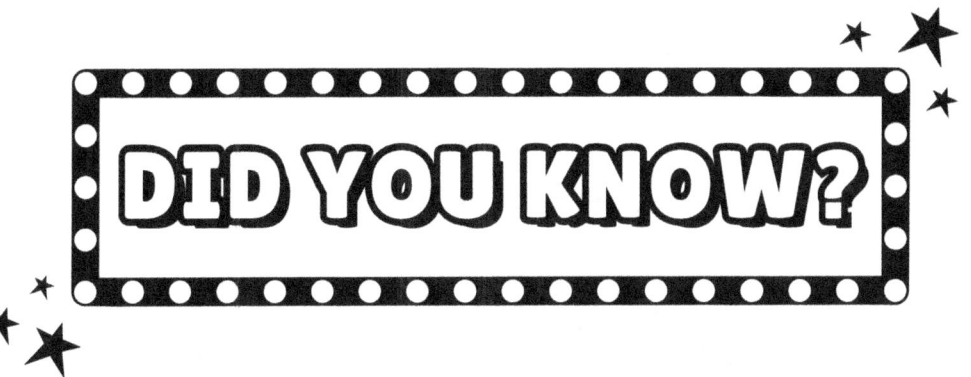

The "British Invasion" of the 1960s was more than just a musical phenomenon. It reshaped fashion, attitudes, and youth culture across the United States. As bands like The Beatles took over the airwaves, they brought a new sense of energy and style that redefined what it meant to be a teenager.

Frank Sinatra, often called "The Chairman of the Board," wasn't just a singer but also a savvy businessman and actor who helped bridge the gap between the Big Band era and modern pop music, paving the way for future crooners.

Jimi Hendrix's innovative guitar techniques, including playing with his teeth and behind his back, shocked audiences, but his groundbreaking use of distortion and feedback forever changed the sound of rock music.

CHAPTER 4

History Highlights

The world has come a long way over the decades; wars were fought and won, leaders rose and fell, and new inventions changed everyday life in ways people never imagined. Some events made front-page headlines; others quietly shaped the future.

This round is all about the big moments, bold moves, and turning points that defined a generation (or two). Let's see how much you remember from history's greatest hits.

1. In 1969, the world watched in awe as a man took his first steps on a dusty, cratered surface far from Earth. What was the name of the Apollo mission that made this moon landing possible?

a) Apollo 11
b) Apollo 13
c) Apollo 10
d) Apollo 1

2. Which U.S. president boldly declared, "Tear down this wall!" near the Berlin Wall in 1987, challenging Soviet leadership during the Cold War?

a) Richard Nixon
b) Ronald Reagan
c) George H.W. Bush
d) Chester W. Nimitz

3. When World War II ended in 1945, which iconic general accepted Japan's formal surrender aboard the *USS Missouri*?

a) George S. Patton
b) Dwight D. Eisenhower
c) Douglas MacArthur
d) Omar Bradley

4. A small, beeping satellite shocked the world and launched the space race between superpowers. When was Sputnik, the first artificial satellite, successfully launched into orbit?

a) 1955
b) 1957
c) 1961
d) 1963

5. This major military operation, launched on June 6, 1944, was a turning point in a global conflict, involving the storming of Normandy's beaches under the codename "Operation Overlord." During which war did this take place?

a) World War I
b) Korean War
c) World War II
d) Vietnam War

6. Which U.S. landmark piece of legislation, signed into law in 1964, outlawed discrimination based on race, color, religion, sex, or national origin?

a) The Voting Rights Act
b) The Civil Rights Act
c) The Equal Pay Act
d) The Emancipation Proclamation

7. The Cuban Missile Crisis of 1962 had the world holding its breath. Which U.S. president was faced with the threat of nuclear war during this thirteen-day standoff?

a) Dwight D. Eisenhower
b) John F. Kennedy

c) Harry S. Truman
d) Lyndon B. Johnson

8. In 1989, a powerful symbol of the Cold War was torn down, signaling the collapse of communist rule in Eastern Europe and paving the way for German reunification. What was this landmark?

a) Berlin Wall
b) Iron Curtain
c) The Western Bloc
d) Great Wall of Germany

9. What was the name of the African-American woman who refused to give up her seat on a bus in 1955, sparking the Montgomery Bus Boycott?

a) Harriet Tubman
b) Rosa Parks
c) Coretta Scott King
d) Maya Angelou

10. The devastating terrorist attacks on September 11, 2001, primarily targeted which two locations in the United States?

a) World Trade Center and the White House
b) The Pentagon and Capitol Building
c) World Trade Center and the Pentagon
d) Times Square and World Trade Center

11. Who delivered the famous "I Have a Dream" speech

at the 1963 March on Washington?

a) Nelson Mandela
b) Malcolm X
c) Martin Luther King Jr.
d) Jesse Jackson

12. Which Cold War conflict, lasting from 1955 to 1975, became one of the most controversial wars in American history?

a) Korean War
b) Vietnam War
c) Gulf War
d) Afghan War

13. What 1971 technological invention revolutionized how people exchanged money and helped spark today's credit card culture?

a) Barcode
b) ATM
c) Internet banking
d) Checkbook

14. In 1948, who became the first prime minister of the newly established nation of Israel?

a) Benjamin Netanyahu
b) Golda Meir
c) David Ben-Gurion
d) Moshe Dayan

15. The United Nations was founded to promote peace after World War II. When was its Charter officially signed?

a) June 26, 1942
b) October 24, 1943
c) June 26, 1945
d) October 24, 1946

16. The Watergate scandal led to the resignation of which U.S. president in 1974?

a) Gerald Ford
b) Richard Nixon
c) Jimmy Carter
d) Lyndon B. Johnson

17. In 1953, which couple was controversially executed in the U.S. for allegedly passing atomic secrets to the Soviet Union?

a) Bonnie and Clyde
b) Julius and Ethel Rosenberg
c) Richard and Pat Nixon
d) Dean and Virginia Acheson

18. Nelson Mandela was released in 1990 and became South Africa's first Black president. How many years was he imprisoned before his release?

a) 18 years
b) 20 years

c) 27 years
d) 32 years

19. What major environmental disaster occurred in 1986, releasing radioactive materials across Europe?

a) Three Mile Island
b) Deepwater Horizon
c) Chernobyl
d) Fukushima

20. In 1972, what historic event marked the first time the U.S. and China formally resumed diplomatic relations after decades of silence?

a) Nixon's visit to Beijing
b) Signing of the U.S.-China Joint Communiqué
c) Establishment of a U.S. Liaison Office in Beijing
d) U.S. support for China's seat at the United Nations

CHAPTER 4 ANSWERS

1. <u>a) Apollo 11</u> - The Apollo 11 mission, led by Neil Armstrong and Buzz Aldrin, made history with the first successful manned moon landing in 1969.

2. <u>b) Ronald Reagan</u> - President Reagan famously challenged Soviet authority with his 1987 speech near the Berlin Wall, urging Gorbachev to "tear down this wall."

3. <u>c) Douglas MacArthur</u> - As Supreme Commander of Allied Forces in the Pacific, MacArthur accepted Japan's surrender aboard the *USS Missouri* in 1945.

4. <u>b) 1957</u> - Sputnik, the first artificial satellite, was launched by the Soviet Union in 1957, marking the start of the space race.

5. <u>c) World War II</u> - Operation Overlord, the codename for D-Day, occurred during World War II and marked a crucial Allied victory.

6. <u>b) The Civil Rights Act</u> - Signed in 1964, this act outlawed discrimination and was a major milestone in the civil rights movement.

7. <u>b) John F. Kennedy</u> - President Kennedy navigated the Cuban Missile Crisis, successfully avoiding nuclear war through diplomacy and naval blockade.

8. <u>a) Berlin Wall</u> - The fall of the Berlin Wall in 1989

symbolized the collapse of communism in Eastern Europe and Germany's reunification.

9. b) Rosa Parks - Rosa Parks' refusal to give up her bus seat in 1955 became a powerful spark for the civil rights movement.

10. c) World Trade Center and the Pentagon - On September 11, 2001, terrorists attacked the Twin Towers and the Pentagon, shocking the world.

11. c) Martin Luther King Jr. - Dr. King delivered his historic "I Have a Dream" speech in 1963, becoming a defining moment of the civil rights era.

12. b) Vietnam War - The Vietnam War was a long and controversial conflict that deeply divided American society and politics.

13. b) ATM - The introduction of the ATM in 1971 revolutionized banking by offering 24/7 access to cash and account services.

14. c) David Ben-Gurion - David Ben-Gurion served as the first Prime Minister of Israel and played a central role in its founding.

15. c) June 26, 1945 - The UN Charter was officially signed in San Francisco on this date, marking the organization's founding.

16. b) Richard Nixon - Facing impeachment over the Watergate scandal, Nixon became the first U.S. president to resign from office in 1974.

17. b) Julius and Ethel Rosenberg - The Rosenbergs were executed for allegedly sharing U.S. nuclear secrets with the Soviet Union during the Cold War.

18. <u>c) 27 years</u> – Nelson Mandela was imprisoned for twenty-seven years before becoming South Africa's first Black president in 1994.

19. <u>c) Chernobyl</u> – The Chernobyl nuclear disaster in 1986 remains one of the worst environmental catastrophes in history.

20. <u>a) Nixon's visit to Beijing</u> – In 1972, President Nixon's groundbreaking visit to China opened diplomatic relations after decades of isolation.

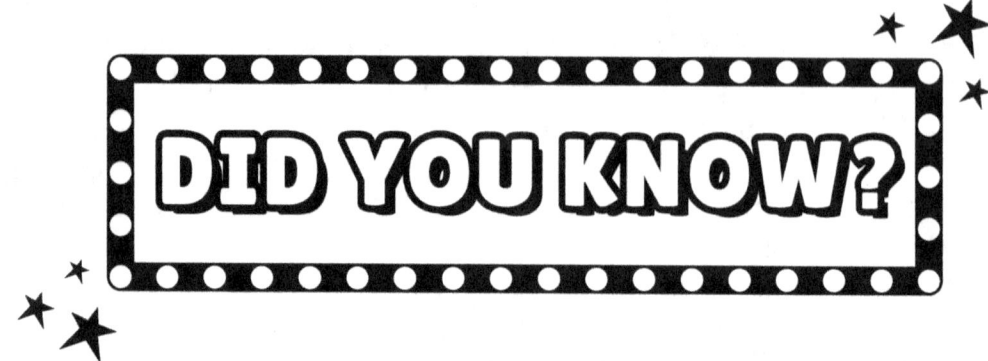

The Berlin Wall was far more than just a wall; it stretched over 100 miles (160 km) and was reinforced with guard towers, barbed wire, and a terrifying "death strip" in between. It became the most visible symbol of the Cold War, splitting families, friends, and a city in two for nearly three decades.

Martin Luther King Jr. didn't originally plan to say "I Have a Dream" in his historic 1963 speech. Encouraged by gospel singer Mahalia Jackson, who shouted, "Tell them about the dream!" he launched into a powerful, unscripted moment that became one of the most iconic speeches in American history.

Neil Armstrong's famous quote as he stepped onto the Moon was meant to say, "That's one small step for a man, one giant leap for mankind." But the "a" was either lost in radio transmission or simply not spoken clearly, forever sparking debate among space historians and linguists.

Gadgets & Tech

From clunky computers to pocket-sized powerhouses, the world of gadgets and technology has changed how we live, work, and play. Remember when cell phones had antennas? Or when the internet made screechy dial-up sounds? From floppy disks to smart assistants, these tech tidbits will take you on a nostalgic (and sometimes surprising) trip through the world of inventions, upgrades, and digital revolutions. Let's see how much you really know about the gadgets that shaped our lives!

1. The first commercially available personal computer, released in 1975, was nicknamed the "Altair 8800." What made this machine especially notable?

a) It had a touchscreen
b) It was sold as a build-it-yourself kit
c) It used voice commands
d) It came preloaded with games

2. Before USB drives became the go-to for portable data, what was the primary medium used to save and transfer computer files in the 1980s and early '90s?

a) Floppy disks
b) Cassette tapes
c) Zip drives
d) Magnetic cards

3. The Nokia 3310, launched in 2000, became legendary for what unexpected reason?

a) It came with the classic game Snake
b) Long-lasting battery life
c) It featured a changeable front cover
d) It could survive being dropped repeatedly

4. The "dial-up" internet sound, a screeching, beeping handshake between your modem and the internet, was once a signature part of logging online. Around what speed did these early connections typically offer?

a) 56 Kbps
b) 128 Kbps
c) 1 Mbps
d) 10 Mbps

5. The phrase "There's an app for that" became popular with the rise of which company's smartphone in the late 2000s?

a) Nokia
b) Apple
c) Blackberry
d) Motorola

6. The Amazon Echo, first launched in 2014, introduced millions of users to what kind of technology?

a) Voice-activated smart assistants
b) Virtual reality
c) Gesture controls
d) Foldable screens

7. In the early 1970s, the world saw the release of the first home video game console, paving the way for decades of gaming innovation. What was the name of this pioneering system?

a) Atari 2600
b) Magnavox Odyssey
c) Nintendo Entertainment System
d) ColecoVision

8. Before the popularity of streaming, what was the dominant way people rented movies for home viewing during the 1990s and early 2000s?

a) VHS tapes
b) LaserDiscs
c) DVDs
d) Blu-ray

9. The term "spam" for unwanted emails actually comes from a famous comedy sketch created by which group or show?

a) *Saturday Night Live*
b) *Monty Python*
c) *The Three Stooges*
d) *The Simpsons*

10. In 1991, the first website was created by Tim Berners-Lee. What was the website's primary purpose?

a) Selling products online
b) Sharing information about the World Wide Web project
c) Social networking
d) Streaming videos

11. Which portable music player revolutionized how people listened to music in the late 1990s and early 2000s, before streaming took over?

a) iPod
b) Walkman
c) Discman
d) Zune

12. The QWERTY keyboard layout was designed in the 19th century to solve what problem?

a) Typists' fingers getting tired too quickly
b) Preventing typewriter keys from jamming
c) Increasing typing speed
d) Making keyboards look more appealing

13. In 2000, the world saw the release of the first commercial camera phone, marking a major shift in mobile technology. Which company was behind it?

a) Sony
b) Nokia
c) Samsung
d) Sharp

14. Though the actual item is nearly obsolete, the floppy disk icon still appears in many software programs today. What does it typically represent?

a) Copy
b) Save
c) Delete
d) Paste

15. What early technology, popular in the 1980s,

allowed users to talk to each other over the phone lines using computers?

a) Text messaging
b) Chat rooms
c) Bulletin board systems (BBS)
d) Internet forums

16. In 1971, the first electronic message was sent between two computers on the same network. Who was responsible for sending this historic email?

a) Ray Tomlinson
b) Bill Gates
c) Steve Jobs
d) Tim Berners-Lee

17. What was the name of the first widely popular web browser, released in 1993?

a) Internet Explorer
b) Netscape Navigator
c) Mosaic
d) Firefox

18. When browsing the internet, you might encounter a "404 Error." What does this error code typically mean?

a) Successful webpage loading
b) Page not found
c) Server crashed
d) Browser outdated

19. Launched in 2007, this device combined a touchscreen, internet access, and sleek design, setting the standard for modern smartphones. Which gadget is credited with starting the smartphone revolution?

a) BlackBerry Bold
b) iPhone
c) HTC Dream
d) Palm Treo

20. Bluetooth technology, used for wireless connections, was named after a 10th-century king from which country?

a) Sweden
b) Denmark
c) Norway
d) Iceland

CHAPTER 5 ANSWERS

1. <u>b) It was sold as a build-it-yourself kit</u> - The Altair 8800 came as a DIY kit, sparking the home computer revolution among hobbyists.

2. <u>a) Floppy disks -</u> These magnetic storage devices were the standard for saving and transferring computer files in the '80s and '90s.

3. <u>d) It could survive being dropped repeatedly</u> - The Nokia 3310 earned a cult following for its legendary durability.

4. <u>a) 56 Kbps</u> - Dial-up modems of the '90s commonly connected at a slow 56 kilobits per second, often with a loud screech.

5. <u>b) Apple</u> - Apple's launch of the iPhone introduced millions to downloadable apps with the catchphrase "There's an app for that."

6. <u>a) Voice-activated smart assistants</u> - The Amazon Echo brought Alexa into homes, making voice-controlled tech mainstream.

7. <u>b) Magnavox Odyssey</u> - Released in 1972, it was the very first home video game console, predating Atari.

8. <u>a) VHS tapes</u> - VHS rentals dominated home entertainment before DVDs and streaming took over.

9. <u>b) Monty Python</u> - The term "spam" was humorously

overused in a *Monty Python* sketch, giving rise to the email term.

10. b) Sharing information about the World Wide Web project - Tim Berners-Lee created the first website to explain how the web worked.

11. a) iPod - Apple's iPod changed how people listened to music, with thousands of songs in your pocket.

12. b) Preventing typewriter keys from jamming - The QWERTY layout spaced out commonly used keys to avoid jams on early typewriters.

13. d) Sharp - Sharp released the first commercial camera phone in Japan, blending photography and mobile calling.

14. b) Save - The floppy disk icon lives on in software as the universal symbol for saving files.

15. c) Bulletin board systems (BBS) - BBSs were early online communities that allowed users to connect and share messages via phone lines.

16. a) Ray Tomlinson - Tomlinson sent the first email in 1971 and introduced the "@" symbol in email addresses.

17. c) Mosaic - Mosaic was the first popular web browser that allowed users to view text and images together.

18. b) Page not found - A 404 error means the webpage you're trying to reach doesn't exist or is broken.

19. b) iPhone - The iPhone's 2007 debut changed

smartphones forever with its sleek touchscreen and app ecosystem.

20. **b) Denmark** - Bluetooth was named after King Harald "Bluetooth" of Denmark, who united tribes like the tech unites devices.

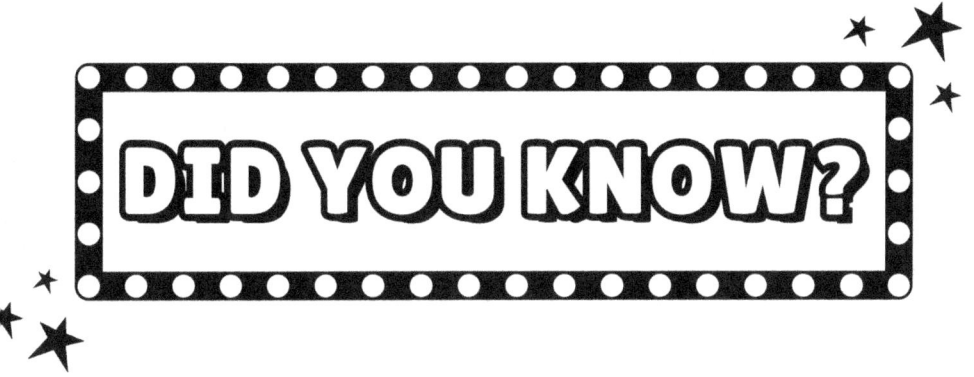

The first camera phone was released in Japan in 1999 and came with a 0.1-megapixel camera. While it might sound primitive today, it marked the beginning of an entirely new way people documented daily life, paving the way for selfies, social media sharing, and the way we use smartphones now.

Early modems made those screeching and beeping sounds because they were using audio tones to transmit digital data over phone lines. These sounds were part of the "handshake" process, where two modems negotiated settings like speed and protocol to establish a stable connection.

Released by Sony in 1979, the Walkman was the first truly portable music player. It let people listen to cassette tapes with headphones while on the go, making music a personal and mobile experience long before digital formats existed.

CHAPTER 6

Sports Legends of the Past

Before social media highlights and million-dollar endorsements, sports heroes made their mark with pure grit, talent, and unforgettable moments. Think of towering home runs, buzzer-beaters, record-breaking runs, and iconic finishes. These legends didn't just play the game, they changed it. Whether on the court, field, track, or ring, their names still echo through stadiums and stories.

Ready to test your knowledge of the greats who made history?

1. Before becoming a baseball legend, in which position did Babe Ruth first make his mark in professional baseball?

a) Catcher
b) Shortstop
c) Pitcher
d) Outfielder

2. Before returning to dominate the NBA again, Michael Jordan surprised the world by briefly pursuing a professional career in which sport?

a) Minor League Baseball
b) Professional Golf
c) European Soccer
d) Arena Football

3. In which year did Jesse Owens famously win four gold medals at the Berlin Olympics, defying Nazi propaganda?

a) 1932
b) 1936
c) 1940
d) 1944

4. The "Miracle on Ice" is remembered as one of the greatest upsets in sports history. Which country's hockey team did the USA defeat in the 1980 Winter Olympics?

a) Canada
b) Sweden
c) Soviet Union
d) Finland

5. Muhammad Ali was known for his poetic trash talk and lightning-fast punches. What was his birth name before he changed it?

a) Cassius Clay
b) Joe Frazier
c) George Foreman
d) Sonny Liston

6. Who was the first female tennis player to win all four Grand Slam titles in a single calendar year, achieving this feat in 1938?

a) Billie Jean King
b) Maureen Connolly
c) Martina Navratilova
d) Suzanne Lenglen

7. Legendary basketball player Wilt Chamberlain once scored 100 points in a single NBA game. In which year did this record-breaking game take place?

a) 1959
b) 1962
c) 1967
d) 1972

8. In soccer history, which player is widely regarded as the "King of Football" and scored over 1,000 career goals?

a) Diego Maradona
b) Pelé
c) Lionel Messi
d) Cristiano Ronaldo

9. The Boston Celtics hold the record for most NBA championships won by a team. How many championships did they win during their dominant run from the 1950s to the 1960s?

a) 9
b) 11
c) 13
d) 15

10. Who was the first African American athlete to break the color barrier in Major League Baseball in 1947?

a) Jackie Robinson
b) Willie Mays
c) Hank Aaron
d) Satchel Paige

11. Which Olympic swimmer won a record-breaking twenty-three gold medals over his career and became an international sensation?

a) Mark Spitz

b) Michael Phelps
c) Ryan Lochte
d) Ian Thorpe

12. Celebrated for his unmatched athletic versatility, Jim Thorpe won two Olympic gold medals in 1912. In which sport did he compete?

a) Swimming
b) Track and Field
c) Boxing
d) Gymnastics

13. The very first Super Bowl was held in 1967, marking the beginning of a new era in professional football. Which two teams faced off in this historic matchup?

a) Dallas Cowboys vs. Green Bay Packers
b) Green Bay Packers vs. Kansas City Chiefs
c) New York Giants vs. Baltimore Colts
d) Pittsburgh Steelers vs. Oakland Raiders

14. Which boxer was famously known as "The Greatest" and had a rivalry dubbed "The Fight of the Century" against Joe Frazier?

a) Rocky Marciano
b) Muhammad Ali
c) Mike Tyson
d) Manny Pacquiao

15. In the 1950s, which gymnast became the first

woman to win Olympic gold in gymnastics, setting the stage for decades of female champions?

a) Olga Korbut
b) Nadia Comăneci
c) Larisa Latynina
d) Věra Čáslavská

16. Which famous cyclist won the Tour de France five times before being stripped of his titles due to doping allegations?

a) Bernard Hinault
b) Miguel Indurain
c) Lance Armstrong
d) Eddy Merckx

17. Barry Bonds, one of the most dominant sluggers in Major League Baseball history, set the all-time career home run record during his twenty-two-season career. How many home runs did he finish with?

a) 714
b) 755
c) 762
d) 701

18. What was the nickname of the legendary Chicago Bulls team during the 1990s, when Michael Jordan led them to six NBA championships?

a) The Dream Team

b) The Showtime Bulls
c) The Bulls Dynasty
d) The Bulls' Second Coming

19. Which NFL player famously rushed for over 2,000 yards in a single season, setting a record that stood for decades?

a) Jim Brown
b) Eric Dickerson
c) Barry Sanders
d) Emmitt Smith

20. In tennis, what historic achievement did Arthur Ashe accomplish in 1968 that broke barriers in the sport?

a) Winning the first U.S. Open open to professionals
b) Becoming the first African American male to win the U.S. Open
c) Winning Wimbledon without losing a set
d) Inventing the "serve and volley" technique

CHAPTER 6 ANSWERS

1. <u>c) Pitcher</u> - Before becoming known for his powerful home runs, Babe Ruth started his professional career as a dominant left-handed pitcher for the Boston Red Sox.

2. <u>a) Minor League Baseball</u> - Michael Jordan temporarily retired from basketball in 1993 to play baseball and joined the Birmingham Barons, a minor league affiliate of the Chicago White Sox.

3. <u>b) 1936</u> - Jesse Owens won four gold medals at the 1936 Berlin Olympics, undermining Adolf Hitler's narrative of racial superiority.

4. <u>c) Soviet Union</u> - In 1980, the U.S. hockey team stunned the heavily favored Soviet Union in the Olympic semi-finals, a true underdog victory.

5. <u>a) Cassius Clay</u> - Muhammad Ali was born Cassius Clay and changed his name after converting to Islam in the 1960s.

6. <u>b) Maureen Connolly</u> - In 1953, Maureen Connolly became the first woman to win all four Grand Slam titles in a single calendar year.

7. <u>b) 1962</u> - Wilt Chamberlain scored a staggering 100 points in a single game against the New York Knicks in 1962.

8. <u>b) Pelé</u> - Brazilian footballer Pelé scored over 1,000

career goals and won three World Cups, earning him the title "King of Football."

9. <u>c) 13</u> - The Celtics won thirteen NBA titles during their dominant stretch in the '50s and '60s, including eight consecutive championships.

10. <u>a) Jackie Robinson</u> - Jackie Robinson broke MLB's color barrier in 1947 with the Brooklyn Dodgers, changing American sports history forever.

11. <u>b) Michael Phelps</u> - Michael Phelps won twenty-three Olympic gold medals, becoming the most decorated Olympian of all time.

12. <u>b) Track and Field -</u> Jim Thorpe won gold medals in both the decathlon and pentathlon at the 1912 Olympics, showcasing extraordinary versatility.

13. <u>b) Green Bay Packers vs. Kansas City Chiefs</u> - The Packers beat the Chiefs in Super Bowl I in 1967, launching the modern era of American football.

14. <u>b) Muhammad Ali</u> - Ali, "The Greatest," had a legendary rivalry with Joe Frazier, including their famous 1971 "Fight of the Century."

15. <u>c) Larisa Latynina</u> - Soviet gymnast Larisa Latynina dominated the 1950s and '60s, winning eighteen Olympic medals in her career.

16. <u>c) Lance Armstrong</u> - Armstrong won the Tour de France seven times before being stripped of his titles for doping violations.

17. <u>c) 762</u> - Barry Bonds hit 762 home runs during his career, the most in MLB history—though not without controversy.

18. c) The Bulls Dynasty - During the '90s, the Chicago Bulls built a dynasty, winning six NBA championships under Michael Jordan's leadership.

19. b) Eric Dickerson - Dickerson rushed for 2,105 yards in 1984, a single-season NFL record that still stands today.

20. b) Becoming the first African American male to win the U.S. Open - In 1968, Arthur Ashe broke racial barriers by becoming the first African American man to win the U.S. Open.

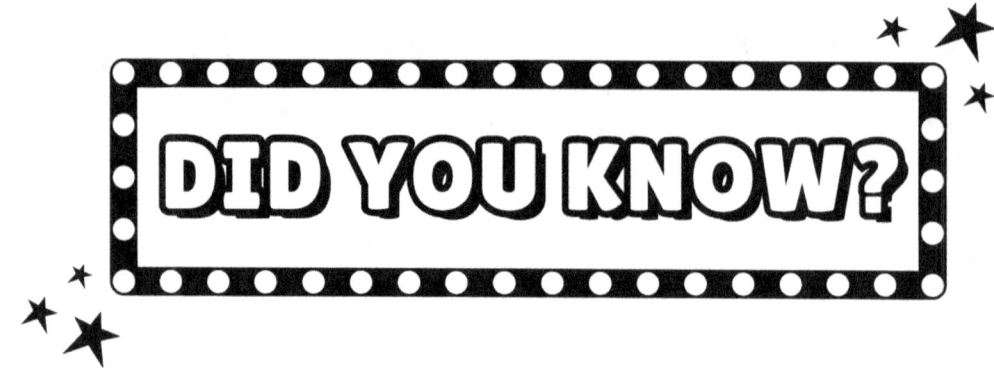

The 1980 Winter Olympics "Miracle on Ice" was one of sports history's most stunning upsets. A young, amateur U.S. hockey team shocked the mighty Soviet Union, the dominant force in the sport, not just winning the game but inspiring a nation with their grit and teamwork during a tense Cold War era.

Muhammad Ali wasn't just a boxer; he was a cultural icon who revolutionized the sport with his unique style. His famous phrase "float like a butterfly, sting like a bee" perfectly described his quick footwork and powerful punches, which combined to make him one of the most captivating athletes of all time.

Maureen Connolly, known as "Little Mo," became the youngest woman to win all four Grand Slam tennis titles in a single year at just eighteen years old. Her remarkable rise was cut short by injury, but her legacy as a trailblazer for women's tennis still shines brightly today.

CHAPTER 7

Retro Toys and Games

Long before touchscreens and digital downloads, fun came in the form of wind-up toys, board games, and action figures. Kids spent hours with Slinkys, Etch A Sketches, and yo-yos, or trading marbles and battling in epic games of Rock 'Em Sock 'Em Robots. Whether you were stacking blocks, solving Rubik's Cubes, or mastering Simon Says, these classic toys brought endless entertainment. Let's see how well you remember the playthings that ruled the playground!

1. Before it became known as the Rubik's Cube, what was the original name given to the puzzle by its Hungarian inventor in 1974?

a) Logic Cube
b) Magic Cube
c) Mastermind Cube
d) Puzzle Cube

2. Released in 1965, this wind-up toy became famous for performing flips and climbs, delighting children around the world. What was this toy called?

a) Tumble Cube
b) Flip Climber
c) Wind-Up Gymnast
d) Jumpin' Jack Cube

3. This electronic game, first released in 1978, challenged players to memorize and repeat increasingly complex sequences of lights and sounds. What was its name?

a) Simon
b) Tamagotchi
c) Lite-Brite
d) Speak & Spell

4. In the classic board game Monopoly, which of the following is an actual rule commonly included in official gameplay?

a) You collect $400 for landing directly on "Go"
b) You must auction any property you land on, but choose not to buy
c) You go straight to jail if you roll doubles three times in a row
d) Both b and c

5. Famous for its glowing artwork and satisfying clicks, which classic toy lets children create colorful designs by inserting translucent pegs into a backlit screen?

a) Lite-Brite
b) Etch A Sketch
c) Magna Doodle
d) Lite Spinners

6. This classic toy, originally marketed in the 1940s, consists of a flexible metal spring that can "walk" down stairs when released. What is it?

a) Slinky
b) Yo-Yo
c) Tinkertoy
d) Lincoln Logs

7. The "Barbie" doll was first introduced by Mattel in what year, quickly becoming a cultural phenomenon and a fixture in toy boxes everywhere?

a) 1959
b) 1965
c) 1971

d) 1948

8. What was the name of the hand-held electronic pet, released in the late 1990s, that required feeding, playing, and care to keep it "alive"?

a) Tamagotchi
b) Furby
c) Poo-Chi
d) DigiPet

9. Released in the 1960s, which game challenges players to carefully remove sticks from a setup without triggering a chaotic fall?

a) Pick-Up Sticks
b) Operation
c) KerPlunk
d) Tipple Tower

10. Known for its high-speed spinning battles and competitive play, which toy became a global craze and inspired tournaments after its debut in the early 2000s?

a) Spin Fighters
b) Beyblade
c) Battle Tops
d) Spin Master Arena

11. Released in 1989, which handheld console became a global sensation and helped popularize portable

gaming, especially with its built-in block-dropping puzzle game?

a) Sega Game Gear
b) Nintendo Game Boy
c) Atari Lynx
d) Milton Bradley Microvision

12. Which classic tabletop game involves guessing words based on one-word clues, encouraging teamwork and creative thinking?

a) Pictionary
b) Taboo
c) Codenames
d) Charades

13. The "Furby," released in 1998, was one of the first toys to interact with users by learning language and responding. What was its most notable feature?

a) Ability to "talk" and learn words
b) It could dance and sing
c) It had a built-in camera
d) It could change colors

14. Which classic children's game, played with marbles, involves aiming and shooting marbles out of a circle?

a) Ringer
b) KerPlunk

c) Marbles Mania
d) Marble Madness

15. In the traditional board game Snakes and Ladders, which of the following rules is actually part of standard gameplay?

a) Rolling a six allows you to climb two ladders
b) Landing on a snake sends you to the nearest snake head
c) You must land exactly on the final square to win
d) Players lose a turn if they climb the same ladder

16. The "Etch A Sketch" was invented in the 1960s by a French electrician who designed it as a mechanical drawing toy. What feature made it unique?

a) Two knobs to draw horizontal and vertical lines
b) A touchscreen surface
c) Magnetic pen and board
d) Digital erasing capability

17. The "Rock 'Em Sock 'Em Robots" game features two robot fighters controlled by players using joysticks. What happens when one robot lands a knockout punch?

a) The robot's head pops up
b) The robot falls over
c) The robot spins around
d) The robot lights up

18. Which spinning toy, often made of wood or plastic, dates back centuries and requires skill to keep it balanced and spinning?

a) Yo-Yo
b) Cup-and-Ball
c) Top
d) Jacob's Ladder

19. Which puzzle game, developed in the 1970s, challenges players to manipulate interlocking shapes in order to form complete lines?

a) Tangram
b) Rubik's Cube
c) Blockout
d) Tetris

20. Which classic puzzle toy, first gaining popularity in the 1980s, features sliding numbered tiles in a square frame and challenges players to restore them to numerical order?

a) Rubik's Clock
b) The 15 Puzzle
c) Perplexus
d) Logic Grid

CHAPTER 7 ANSWERS

1. <u>b) Magic Cube</u> - Before it became the Rubik's Cube, Ernő Rubik called it the "Magic Cube" when he invented it in 1974.

2. <u>d) Jumpin' Jack Cube</u> - A popular wind-up toy in the '60s, Jumpin' Jack Cube was loved for its flipping, climbing tricks.

3. <u>a) Simon</u> - Simon tested memory by flashing colored lights in a sequence you had to repeat, harder each round.

4. <u>d) Both b and b</u> - According to official Monopoly rules, unpurchased properties must be auctioned, and rolling three doubles in a row sends you to jail.

5. <u>a) Lite-Brite</u> - Kids used Lite-Brite to push colored pegs into a glowing board, creating pictures that lit up.

6. <u>a) Slinky</u> - The metal spring known as the Slinky could walk down stairs and became a classic toy in the 1940s.

7. <u>a) 1959</u> - Barbie made her debut in 1959 and became a fashion icon and best-selling doll worldwide.

8. <u>a) Tamagotchi</u>- Tamagotchis were tiny digital pets that needed feeding, playing, and care to stay alive.

9. c) KerPlunk - In KerPlunk, players pull sticks from a tube without dropping marbles—a fun game of balance and luck.

10. b) Beyblade - Beyblades were spinning battle tops that became a global sensation in the early 2000s.

11. a) Nintendo Game Boy - The Game Boy launched in 1989 with Tetris and helped make portable gaming a huge trend.

12. c) Codenames - Codenames uses one-word clues to help teammates guess the right words.

13. a) Two knobs to draw horizontal and vertical lines - Etch A Sketch used two knobs to draw lines, letting kids create pictures with no ink or mess.

14. a) The robot's head pops up - In Rock 'Em Sock 'Em Robots, a perfect punch pops the opponent's head up, winning the round.

15. c) Top - Spinning tops have existed for centuries, offering simple fun through motion and balance.

16. d) Tetris - Tetris challenged players to stack falling shapes into complete lines—a puzzle classic.

17. a) Ability to "talk" and learn words - Furby was one of the first interactive toys that responded to users and learned speech over time.

18. a) Ringer - In Ringer, kids flicked marbles to knock others out of a circle and win them.

19. c) You must land exactly on the final square to win - In Snakes and Ladders, players must roll the exact number to finish the game.

20. b) The 15 Puzzle - This sliding tile puzzle required logic to arrange numbers 1-15 in order using one empty space.

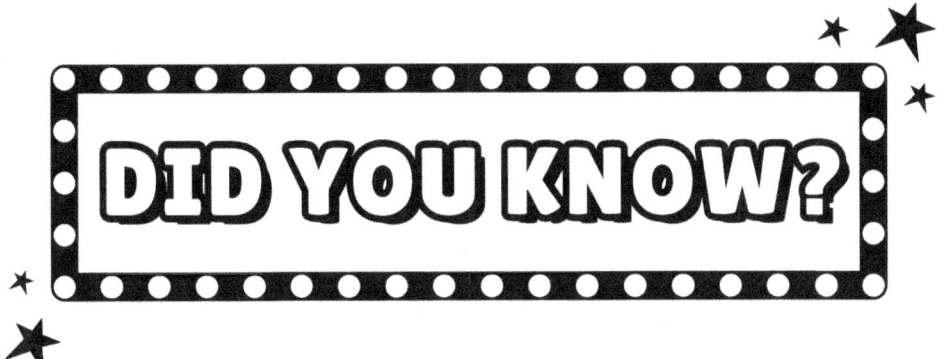

The Rubik's Cube has over forty-three quintillion possible configurations, making it one of the most complex handheld puzzles ever created. Invented in 1974 by Hungarian professor Ernő Rubik, it can be solved in twenty moves or fewer using optimized algorithms, a feat speedcubers worldwide continue to master today.

The original Slinky was invented by accident in 1943 by naval engineer Richard James, who was working with tension springs for ship equipment. When one fell off his desk, he noticed it appeared to "walk" down instead of dropping straight to the floor, inspiring the creation of one of the most enduring toys of all time.

Simon, the colorful memory game, was created in 1978 by Ralph H. Baer, often referred to as the "Father of Video Games." The toy challenged players to repeat increasingly complex sequences of tones and lights, and its musical structure helped shape early electronic game sound design.

CHAPTER 8

School Days

Remember when desks had flip-up lids and teachers wheeled in TVs for filmstrips? Whether it was sharpening your pencil to delay a test or passing notes behind textbooks, school life from the 1950s to the 1960s had its unforgettable rhythms. Let's take attendance and see how well you remember your classroom days!

1. What was a common feature on school classroom walls in the 1950s during Cold War tensions?

a) A map of Europe
b) The Ten Commandments
c) A civil defense air raid poster
d) A multiplication chart

2. Before mechanical pencils became common, what did many students use to carry and protect their wooden pencils?

a) Metal case
b) Canvas roll
c) Pencil box
d) Snap-top pouch

3. What kind of film was often shown in school to teach students about safety, hygiene, or manners during the 1950s and 1960s?

a) Public television broadcasts
b) Informational slideshows
c) Educational filmstrips
d) Weekly news

4. Before electronic calculators became common, which handheld device was widely used in classrooms to perform mathematical calculations?

a) Graphing board
b) Slide rule

c) Punch card
d) Math wheel

5. At many schools, what weekly event brought students
together in the gym or cafeteria for announcements, presentations, or special screenings?

a) Home Ec hour
b) School showcase
c) Assembly
d) Study hall

6. What item did students frequently cover in brown paper bags or decorative wrapping to protect it throughout the year?

a) Binder
b) Report Card
c) Textbook
d) Notebook

7. What large, mechanical item in school offices was used to make copies before photocopiers became mainstream?

a) Thermofax
b) Mimeograph machine
c) Duplicator press
d) Carbon roll printer

8. In many schools during the '60s, what special

program took students out of class for dental hygiene education?

a) Smile Day
b) Fluoride Fridays
c) Tooth Talk
d) Dental Bus

9. Which subject often included learning cursive handwriting, sentence structure, and parts of speech?

a) Language Arts
b) Social Studies
c) Penmanship
d) Composition

10. What classroom ritual involved students standing beside their desks and reciting a patriotic statement each morning?

a) The School Creed
b) Morning Prayer
c) The Pledge of Allegiance
d) The Honor Oath

11. What was the name of the elementary school-level math program known for its cartoon mascots and workbooks?

a) Number Ninjas
b) Math-a-Magics
c) Math Blasters

d) Schoolhouse Rock

12. In traditional classrooms before whiteboards took over, what tool was commonly used to clean writing surfaces, often leaving behind a dusty trail?

a) Chalk wiper
b) Felt eraser
c) Blackboard sponge
d) Dust cloth

13. What piece of classroom furniture had an attached writing surface and a cubbyhole underneath for storing books?

a) Writing bench
b) Arm desk
c) Lift-top desk
d) Combo desk

14. What was the standard method for playing music or instructional audio in most classrooms during the 1950s?

a) Wax cylinder player
b) Classroom phonograph
c) Tape deck with reel-to-reel
d) Audio slide carousel system

15. What classroom item was used to keep ink ready for fountain pens before ballpoint pens became common?

a) Ink cartridge
b) Ink sponge
c) Inkwell
d) Pen nib jar

16. What kind of shoes were part of many students' everyday outfits during the 1950s school year?

a) Oxford walkers
b) Saddle shoes
c) Penny loafers
d) Buckled flats

17. In the 1950s, how did many students learn U.S. geography in class?

a) Cardboard map puzzles
b) Pull-down wall maps and globes
c) Atlas radio broadcasts
d) Flipbook atlases with overlays

18. What was the most common way teachers got students' attention in a noisy 1960s classroom?

a) Flashing lights
b) Tapping a ruler or pointer on the desk
c) Whistle
d) Clapping pattern

19. What classroom tool was widely used for writing math problems and spelling words during lessons?

a) Slate boards with chalk trays
b) Paper scroll charts with wax pencils
c) Dry-erase boards
d) Cardboards with grease pencils

20. What kind of lunch container did many kids bring to school in the 1950s?

a) Insulated paper bags
b) Plastic bento boxes
c) Metal lunch boxes with cartoon designs
d) Disposable containers

CHAPTER 8 ANSWERS

1. <u>c) A civil defense air raid poster</u> – During the Cold War, many classrooms displayed air raid instructions as part of civil defense drills.

2. <u>c) Pencil box</u> – Pencil boxes were common for neatly storing pencils, erasers, and sharpeners before the days of plastic cases.

3. <u>c) Educational filmstrips</u> – Filmstrips with narration were used widely in classrooms to teach life skills and subject lessons.

4. <u>b) Slide rule</u> – Before calculators, the slide rule was a standard tool for solving math and engineering problems.

5. <u>c) Assembly</u> – Weekly assemblies were a school tradition, featuring announcements, performances, or educational programs.

6. <u>c) Textbook</u> – Students wrapped textbooks in paper covers to protect them, as books were often reused yearly.

7. <u>b) Mimeograph machine</u> – Mimeographs made copies using ink and stencils, leaving that signature purple text on worksheets.

8. <u>b) Fluoride Fridays</u> – Many schools partnered with health departments to provide fluoride treatments for dental hygiene.

9. c) Penmanship – Penmanship classes emphasized cursive writing, proper spacing, and neat handwriting.

10. c) The Pledge of Allegiance – Reciting the pledge was a daily routine in many American classrooms starting in the 1950s.

11. d) Schoolhouse Rock – This animated series combined catchy songs with educational topics like math and grammar.

12. b) Felt eraser – Chalkboards were cleaned with thick felt erasers, which often left clouds of chalk dust.

13. d) Combo desk – The combo desk featured a seat with an attached writing surface and storage underneath.

14. b) Classroom phonograph - In the 1950s, schools commonly used phonographs to play vinyl records for music education, language lessons, and storytelling.

15. c) Inkwell – Inkwells were built into many student desks so children could dip their fountain pens before ballpoint pens became widespread.

16. c) Saddle shoes – These distinctive two-tone shoes were especially popular with schoolchildren and often worn with skirts or slacks.

17. b) Pull-down wall maps and globes – Geography lessons relied heavily on pull-down maps and classroom globes to explore states and countries.

18. b) Tapping a ruler or pointer on the desk – A sharp tap from a wooden pointer was a common way for teachers to restore order quickly.

19. <u>d) Large blackboard at the front of the room</u> – Before whiteboards, teachers used blackboards for most visual teaching, often with chalk and erasers.

20. <u>c) Metal lunch boxes with cartoon designs</u> – These sturdy boxes, often featuring comic book heroes or TV characters, were lunch essentials for kids.

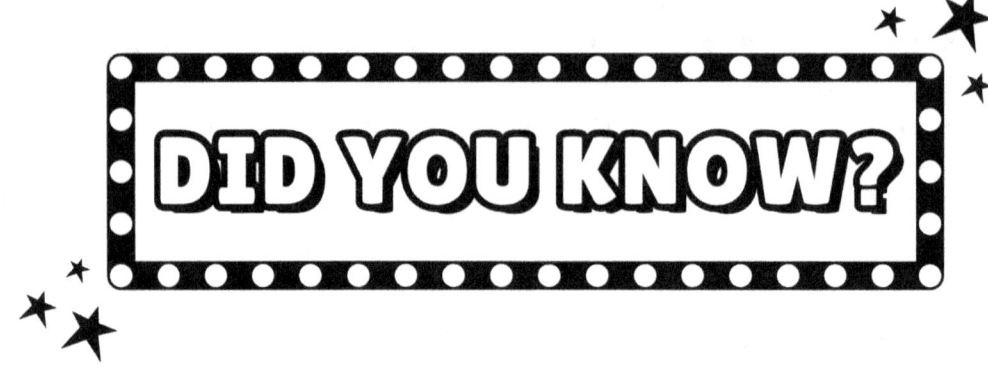

In the 1950s and 1960s, many classrooms appointed "school monitors"—students selected by the teacher to help maintain order, distribute supplies, erase the blackboard, or lead lines to the cafeteria or playground. These roles were considered a privilege, and monitors often wore fabric armbands, pins, or badges to show their status.

Before digital clocks became common, teachers used oversized analog "teaching clocks" in the classroom to help students learn how to tell time. These clocks had movable hour and minute hands that could be adjusted by the teacher, making them a hands-on visual aid for young learners during math and daily routine lessons.

Before personal pencil sharpeners were common, many classrooms had a wall-mounted crank sharpener, usually placed near the blackboard or door. These metal devices made a loud grinding sound as students took turns sharpening their pencils—often using it as a quick break from class.

Famous People

Some names are more than just names; they're moments in history. Whether they made headlines, broke records, inspired movements, or stole the spotlight on stage or screen, these iconic figures left a mark that's still talked about today. Think of world leaders, movie stars, inventors, and trailblazers from all walks of life. You've heard the names, now let's see what you really know about the people who helped shape the world!

1. Before becoming a central figure in the civil rights movement, Martin Luther King Jr. pursued advanced academic studies. In which field did he earn his doctoral degree?

a) Theology
b) Law
c) History
d) Sociology

2. Which groundbreaking artist rose to fame in the 1950s by blending gospel, blues, and country influences into a new sound that helped launch the rock and roll era?

a) Buddy Holly
b) Chuck Berry
c) Jerry Lee Lewis
d) Elvis Presley

3. Marie Curie was the first woman to win a Nobel Prize, but in which two scientific fields did she earn this rare honor?

a) Physics and Chemistry
b) Medicine and Chemistry
c) Physics and Biology
d) Chemistry and Medicine

4. Known for his inventions and scientific genius, which American inventor famously created the phonograph and improved the light bulb?

a) Thomas Edison
b) Nikola Tesla
c) Alexander Graham Bell
d) Benjamin Franklin

5. Which British writer, once a struggling single parent, created a fictional world centered around a hidden school of magic, secret spells, and a boy destined to challenge a dark wizard?

a) J.R.R. Tolkien
b) J.K. Rowling
c) C.S. Lewis
d) Philip Pullman

6. Before becoming a symbol of the civil rights movement, Rosa Parks held which important position within the Montgomery chapter of the NAACP (National Association for the Advancement of Colored People)?

a) Treasurer
b) Youth Advisor
c) Public Speaker
d) Secretary

7. During a time of deep economic crisis, which U.S. president sought to calm the nation by declaring, "The only thing we have to fear is fear itself" in his 1933 inaugural address?

a) Harry Truman

b) Theodore Roosevelt
c) Franklin D. Roosevelt
d) Woodrow Wilson

8. In 1932, which pioneering female aviator made history by flying solo and nonstop across the Atlantic Ocean, becoming an international icon?

a) Harriet Quimby
b) Jacqueline Cochran
c) Bessie Coleman
d) Amelia Earhart

9. Before becoming South Africa's first Black president, which of the following roles did Nelson Mandela hold?

a) United Nations ambassador for human rights
b) Co-founder of the Pan African Congress
c) Defense attorney fighting apartheid laws
d) President of the South African Communist Party

10. Known for his role as a civil rights lawyer and the first African American Supreme Court Justice, who was he?

a) Thurgood Marshall
b) Clarence Thomas
c) Sonia Sotomayor
d) Barack Obama

11. Which award-winning actress, known for her intelligence and early start in Hollywood, earned an

Oscar for playing an FBI trainee in a psychological thriller and has also spoken out in support of youth education?

a) Meryl Streep
b) Nicole Kidman
c) Jodie Foster
d) Cate Blanchett

12. The Beatles left an unforgettable mark on music history. Which of the band's members was fatally shot outside his New York City residence in 1980, shocking fans around the world?

a) John Lennon
b) Paul McCartney
c) George Harrison
d) Ringo Starr

13. Who was the famous physicist who developed the theory of general relativity, changing the way we understand gravity?

a) Albert Einstein
b) Isaac Newton
c) Galileo Galilei
d) Stephen Hawking

14. Known as the "Iron Lady," who was the first female Prime Minister of the United Kingdom?

a) Margaret Thatcher

b) Theresa May
c) Angela Merkel
d) Indira Gandhi

15. Which event led to Martin Luther King Jr. becoming the youngest recipient of the Nobel Peace Prize in 1964?

a) His work in organizing the Selma marches
b) His leadership during the Montgomery Bus Boycott
c) His nonviolent resistance during the Freedom Rides
d) His role in founding the Southern Christian Leadership Conference (SCLC)

16. Which iconic artist, celebrated for her deeply personal self-portraits and bold imagery, became a symbol of strength, culture, and identity?

a) Frida Kahlo
b) Pablo Picasso
c) Andy Warhol
d) Salvador Dalí

17. Which boxer became the youngest heavyweight champion in history at age twenty, known for his explosive power and controversial career both inside and outside the ring?

a) Evander Holyfield
b) Floyd Mayweather Jr.
c) Mike Tyson
d) Lennox Lewis

18. Which legendary artist, known for his emotional struggles and vivid brushstrokes, once mutilated part of his own body during a mental health crisis?

a) Salvador Dalí
b) Vincent van Gogh
c) Pablo Picasso
d) Henri Matisse

19. Before becoming an astronaut, Neil Armstrong served as a test pilot and flew combat missions during which war?

a) Vietnam War
b) Korean War
c) World War II
d) Gulf War

20. Which South African leader, awarded the Nobel Peace Prize, became an international voice of moral leadership and reconciliation during the fight against apartheid?

a) Steve Biko
b) Desmond Tutu
c) Nelson Mandela
d) Thabo Mbeki

CHAPTER 9 ANSWERS

1. <u>a) Theology</u> - Martin Luther King Jr. earned his Ph.D. in systematic theology from Boston University in 1955.

2. <u>d) Elvis Presley</u> - Presley revolutionized music in the 1950s by blending blues, gospel, and country into rock and roll.

3. <u>a) Physics and Chemistry</u> - Marie Curie remains the only person to win Nobel Prizes in both physics (1903) and chemistry (1911).

4. <u>a) Thomas Edison</u> - Edison invented the phonograph and greatly improved the incandescent light bulb, shaping modern life.

5. <u>b) J.K. Rowling</u> - Rowling created the *Harry Potter* series, building an enduring magical world starting in the 1990s.

6. <u>d) Secretary</u> - Rosa Parks served as the NAACP secretary, a key role that supported the civil rights organization and action.

7. <u>c) Franklin D. Roosevelt</u> - FDR's famous 1933 quote sought to uplift Americans during the depths of the Great Depression.

8. <u>d) Amelia Earhart</u> - In 1932, Earhart became the first woman to fly solo across the Atlantic, inspiring generations.

9. c) Defense attorney fighting apartheid laws - Mandela defended Black South Africans in court before his activism turned revolutionary.

10. a) Thurgood Marshall - Marshall argued Brown v. Board of Education and became the first Black Supreme Court justice.

11. c) Jodie Foster - Foster won an Oscar for *The Silence of the Lambs* and advocates for education and youth programs.

12. a) John Lennon - Lennon's tragic death in 1980 shocked fans and marked the end of an era for The Beatles admirers.

13. a) Albert Einstein - Einstein's general theory of relativity transformed our understanding of gravity and the universe.

14. a) Margaret Thatcher - Thatcher served from 1979 to 1990 and was known for her strong conservative leadership.

15. b) His leadership during the Montgomery Bus Boycott - King's guidance in the 1955 boycott brought him national attention.

16. a) Frida Kahlo - She is known for her powerful self-portraits that reflect pain, identity, and Mexican culture, making her an enduring icon in both art and activism.

17. c) Mike Tyson - Tyson shocked the sports world by becoming heavyweight champion at just twenty years old.

18. d) Vincent van Gogh - In 1888, Van Gogh famously

cut off part of his ear during a mental health crisis.

19. b) Korean War - Before joining NASA, Armstrong flew fighter jets during the Korean War.

20. b) Desmond Tutu - Tutu won the Nobel Peace Prize in 1984 for his peaceful resistance to apartheid in South Africa.

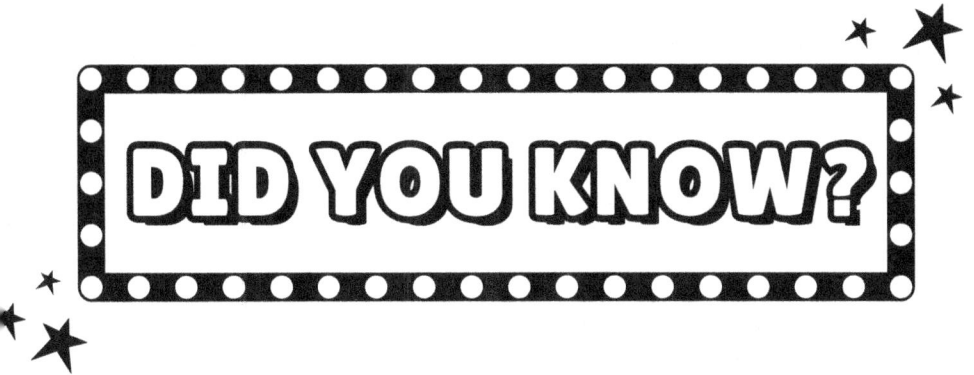

Thomas Edison was a prolific inventor who held over 1,000 patents in his lifetime. His inventions, like the phonograph and improvements to the electric light bulb, helped transform everyday life in the late 19th and early 20th centuries, laying the foundation for the modern electrical age and entertainment industry.

J.K. Rowling's journey to success was far from easy. After multiple rejections by publishers, her first *Harry Potter* book was finally accepted and became a global phenomenon, inspiring millions of readers and sparking a cultural movement centered around magic, friendship, and courage.

Marie Curie remains the only person to win Nobel Prizes in two different sciences; Physics in 1903 (for her work on radioactivity) and Chemistry in 1911 (for discovering the elements polonium and radium). She conducted much of her research under harsh, makeshift lab conditions, and her pioneering efforts opened the door for modern nuclear science.

Food and Drink

Before food delivery apps and fancy lattes, meals were simpler but full of flavor and heart. A cold bottle of cola from the corner store, mom's meatloaf on a weeknight, or that one candy you'd trade your whole lunch for, those bites stick in your memory. Snack time, dinnertime, anytime, every era had its favorites. Let's dig in and see how many tasty tidbits you remember from the good old days!

1. Originally marketed as a health tonic and temperance-friendly drink in the early 20th century, which fizzy beverage gained massive popularity despite early controversy over its ingredients?

a) Sarsaparilla
b) Root Beer
c) Coca-Cola
d) Ginger Tonic

2. The invention of the sandwich is often credited to an 18th-century English nobleman who wanted a quick meal that wouldn't interrupt his card games. What was this nobleman's title?

a) Earl of Sandwich
b) Duke of Suffolk
c) Viscount of Brixton
d) Baron of Sandwich

3. Which fruit, now a staple in American pies and desserts, was once considered a luxury item only affordable to the wealthy during the colonial era?

a) Apples
b) Blueberries
c) Strawberries
d) Cranberries

4. The popular mid-century American dinner staple "TV dinner" was introduced in the 1950s to cater to the growing culture of watching television at home. Which

company pioneered this convenient frozen meal concept?

a) Swanson
b) Campbell's
c) Stouffer's
d) Kraft

5. Though often associated with Italy, pizza's rise to worldwide fame truly skyrocketed after which major historical event that brought soldiers home craving new flavors?

a) World War I
b) The Great Depression
c) World War II
d) The Cold War

6. Which classic American dish, often made with ground beef and mashed potatoes, was created as an economical and filling meal during the hardships of the Great Depression?

a) Shepherd's pie
b) Meatloaf
c) Beef stew
d) Meatball

7. The peanut butter and jelly sandwich became an iconic American snack in the 20th century. But peanut butter itself was first developed in which decade?

a) 1880s
b) 1900s
c) 1920s
d) 1940s

8. Before electric refrigerators were common, what was the primary method for preserving fresh milk and dairy products at home?

a) Canning
b) Ice boxes packed with ice
c) Fermentation
d) Drying

9. Which post-war food product, first sold nationally in the 1950s, was marketed as a "miracle meat" and became a staple in lunchboxes and military rations?

a) Deviled Ham
b) Luncheon Meat
c) Vienna Sausage
d) Potted Meat

10. Which carbonated beverage, first marketed in the late 19th century as a medicinal tonic, quickly rose in popularity due to its unique formula and bold marketing?

a) Pepsi
b) Dr Pepper
c) Coca-Cola
d) 7-Up

11. Which snack food, originally sold by street vendors, gained massive popularity in entertainment venues during the early 1900s and is now closely tied to the movie-going experience?

a) Potato chips
b) Pretzels
c) Popcorn
d) Roasted peanuts

12. Which type of cheese, beloved in many American households, is known for its bright orange color and mild flavor, often melted on burgers and sandwiches?

a) Swiss
b) Cheddar
c) American processed cheese
d) Mozzarella

13. The concept of "happy hour," featuring discounted drinks and appetizers, first gained popularity during which decade in American bars?

a) 1920s
b) 1950s
c) 1970s
d) 1990s

14. This wobbly, brightly colored dessert was a staple at 1950s parties, often molded into elaborate shapes. What was the primary thickening ingredient that gave it its iconic jiggle?

a) Agar
b) Gelatin powder
c) Pectin
d) Cornstarch

15. In the 1940s, what type of powdered drink mix gained popularity among American families for being affordable, easy to store, and marketed as nutritious for kids?

a) Nestlé Milo
b) Nesquik
c) Tang
d) Ovaltine

16. Which shelf-stable product, introduced in the 1950s, was often used to make quick casseroles and is still recognized today by its iconic red-and-white can?

a) Canned pumpkin
b) Creamed celery soup
c) Condensed cream of mushroom soup
d) Tomato paste

17. Before being widely sold in grocery stores, which type of bread was commonly baked fresh daily by local bakeries and sold in paper bags?

a) White sandwich bread
b) Rye bread
c) Sourdough

d) Whole wheat

18. Which kitchen appliance, widely adopted in American households during the 1940s and 1950s, helped modernize cooking by providing more consistent temperature control and cleaner operation than traditional stoves?

a) Enamel gas cooker
b) Induction plate
c) Electric range
d) Rotary oven

19. The classic American hot dog, often served at baseball games and barbecues, originated from immigrants from which European country?

a) Germany
b) Italy
c) France
d) Austria

20. What popular sweet treat, made from sugar and corn syrup, became widely available after World War II and was often enjoyed at carnivals and fairs?

a) Cotton candy
b) Fudge
c) Taffy
d) Caramel apples

CHAPTER 10 ANSWERS

1. <u>c) Coca-Cola</u> - First sold in 1886, Coca-Cola was originally marketed as a medicinal tonic but grew to become a global soft drink brand.

2. <u>a) Earl of Sandwich</u> - John Montagu, the 4th Earl of Sandwich, is credited with creating the sandwich so he could eat without leaving the card table.

3. <u>a) Apples</u> - During colonial times, apples were expensive and often imported or grown with difficulty, making them a luxury fruit.

4. <u>a) Swanson</u> - Swanson coined the term "TV dinner" in 1953, packaging frozen meals in trays to match the rise of television culture.

5. <u>c) World War II</u> - After WWII, returning U.S. soldiers craved the pizza they had discovered in Italy, helping spread its popularity in America.

6. <u>b) Meatloaf</u> - A Depression-era dish, meatloaf combined affordable ingredients to create a hearty, economical meal for families.

7. <u>a) 1880s</u> - Peanut butter was first developed in the 1880s as a protein-rich food for people who couldn't chew meat.

8. <u>b) Ice boxes packed with ice</u> - Before refrigeration, households used insulated ice boxes to keep milk and

perishables cool.

9. **b) Luncheon Meat** - Luncheon meat, especially Spam, became popular in the 1950s for its convenience, long shelf life, and use in military rations and everyday meals.

10. **c) Coca-Cola** - With its secret formula and bold marketing, Coca-Cola became a cultural icon far beyond its medicinal beginnings.

11. **c) Popcorn** - Popcorn surged in popularity during the early 20th century as a cheap and fun snack, especially at movie theaters.

12. **c) American processed cheese** - Known for its meltability and bright color, this cheese became a staple in sandwiches and fast food.

13. **b) 1950s** - "Happy hour" began to catch on in American bars in the 1950s as a way to draw in crowds before dinner service.

14. **b) Gelatin powder** - Gelatin, made from animal collagen, gives Jell-O and similar desserts their signature jiggly texture.

15. **b) Condensed cream of mushroom soup** - Campbell's cream of mushroom soup became a key ingredient in 1950s casseroles like green bean casserole, often dubbed "America's béchamel."

16. **c) Ovaltine** - Ovaltine was promoted as a healthy bedtime drink and gained widespread popularity thanks to its tie-ins with children's radio programs and school campaigns.

17. **a) White sandwich bread** - Before industrial

production, fresh white bread was delivered daily by bakeries and sold in paper wrapping.

18. c) Electric range - Electric ranges became widely adopted in American homes during the 1940s and 1950s, offering a cleaner, more modern alternative to wood or gas stoves.

19. a) Germany - The American hot dog traces back to German immigrants who brought over sausages like frankfurters and wieners.

20. a) Cotton candy - Invented in the 19th century but popularized after WWII, cotton candy became a fairground favorite thanks to its light, sugary texture.

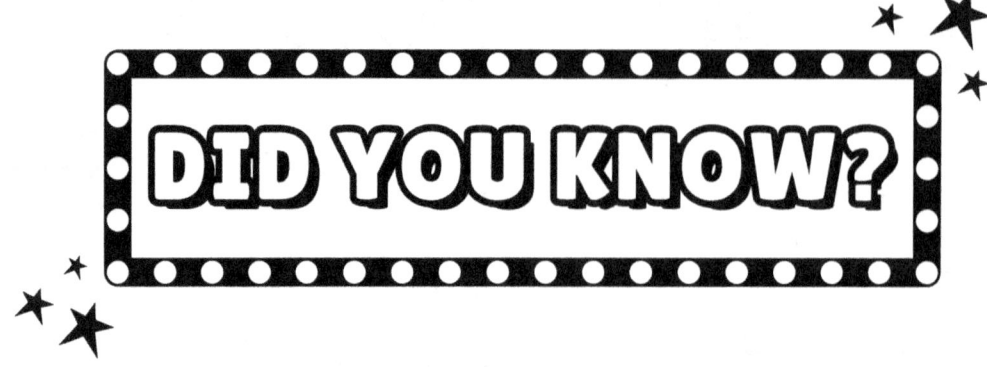

Though pizza had existed in immigrant communities, it was returning soldiers from Italy after World War II who craved the flavors they discovered abroad. This demand helped transform pizza into a mainstream American favorite by the 1950s.

Popcorn exploded in popularity during the Great Depression because it cost only five to ten cents a bag, making it one of the few affordable luxuries. Movie theaters capitalized on this by selling popcorn in the lobbies, and by the 1940s, the buttery snack had become permanently linked with the movie-going experience.

Peanut butter was first introduced in the 1880s as a health food designed for people who had difficulty chewing, like the elderly or patients recovering from illness. It wasn't sweetened or marketed to children until the 1920s, when companies like Skippy and Jif helped turn it into the lunchbox staple we know today.

CONCLUSION

You did it!

And just like that, you've made it to the end of your 80th Birthday Trivia Challenge. Whether you knew every answer or just enjoyed taking a walk down memory lane, I hope it brought a smile to your face and a few fun stories to mind.

Looking back on eight decades is no small thing. You've lived through some of the most incredible moments in history, witnessed amazing changes, and gathered countless memories along the way. This little book is just a small celebration of all that you've seen, done, and become.

I hope it sparked laughter, surprise, and maybe even a few "Hey, I remember that!" moments. But more than anything, I hope it reminded you just how rich and full your journey has been.

So here's to you, your life, your stories, and your eighty wonderful years. May the years ahead be filled with love, good health, and many more moments to celebrate.

Happy 80th Birthday!

Thanks for reading!

Thanks for picking up this book! As a special thank-you, I've lined up some awesome freebies for you:

• 500 World War I & II Facts — digital edition
• 101 Idioms and Phrases — digital edition
• 1144 Random Facts — full audiobook

Scan the QR code below, enter your email, and all three bonuses will be on their way. Enjoy your extra content!